SCHOLASTIC

EARLY YEARS

PHOTOCOPIABLES

Communication, Language and Literacy

INCLUDES CD-ROM WITH OVER 100 ACTIVITIES

- COVERS FIVE FAVOURITE THEMES -
- EARLY LEARNING GOALS • DIFFERENTIATED ACTIVITIES -

© 2006 Scholastic Ltd

Designed using Adobe InDesign

Published by Scholastic Ltd
Villiers House
Clarendon Avenue
Leamington Spa
Warwickshire CV32 5PR

www.scholastic.co.uk

Printed by Bell & Bain

123456789   6789012345

British Library Cataloguing-in-Publication Data
A catalogue record for this book is available from the British Library.

ISBN 0-439-96545-4
ISBN 978-0439-96545-3

The rights of the authors of this work have been asserted by them in accordance with the Copyright, Designs and Patents Act 1988. Extracts from The National Literacy Strategy © Crown copyright. Reproduced under the terms of HMSO Guidance Note 8.

All rights reserved. This book is sold subject to the condition that it shall not, by way of trade or otherwise, be lent, hired out or otherwise circulated without the publisher's prior consent in any form of binding or cover other than that in which it is published and without a similar condition, including this condition, being imposed upon the subsequent purchaser.

No part of this publication may be reproduced, stored in a retrieval system, or transmitted, in any form or by any means, electronic, mechanical, photocopying, recording or otherwise, without the prior permission of the publisher. This book remains copyright, although permission is granted to copy pages where indicated for classroom distribution and use only in the school which has purchased the book, or by the teacher who has purchased the book, and in accordance with the CLA licensing agreement. Photocopying permission is given only for purchasers and not for borrowers of books from any lending service.

Credits

Series Editor Sally Gray
Assistant Editor Andrea Lewis
Series Designer Anna Oliwa
Designer Andrea Lewis

Acknowledgements

The publishers gratefully acknowledge permission to reproduce the following copyright material:

Text
© Lesley Clark: p32, p42
© Sally Gray: p3, p4, p5, p8, p9, p10, p16, p17, p25, p26, p28, p29, p31, p33, p34, p35, p40, p41, p43, p52, p53, p55, p56
© Chris Heald: p6, p7, p51
© Pauline Kenyon: p15, p62
© Barbara J Leach: p54
© Dr Hannah Mortimer: p20, p21, p22, p23, p30, p60, p61
© Jenni Tavener: p13, p14, p18, p19, p36, p44, p46, p48, p49, p50, p63
© Brenda Williams: p11, p12, p24
© Irene Yates: p27, p37, p38, p39, p45, p46, p57, p58, p59

Illustrations
© Claire Boyce: p15, p62
© Terry Burton: p6, p7, p51
© Lynne Farmer: p13, p14, p18, p19, p47, p48, p49, p50, p63
© Cathy Hughes: p20, p21, p22, p30, p60, p61
© Lynda Murray: p32, p42
© Angie Sage: p8, p23, p33, p34, p35, p43, p55, p56
© Jessica Stockham: p11, p12, p24, p36, p44
© Sami Sweeten: p54
© Jenny Tulip: p9, p10, p25, p26, p27, p31, p37, p38, p39, p45, p46, p57, p58, p59

Every effort has been made to trace copyright holders and the publishers apologise for any inadvertent omissions.

Contents

PAGE 3 Introduction

PAGE 4 Stories and rhymes
4 Teacher's notes
6 Photocopiables

PAGE 16 Ourselves
16 Teacher's notes
18 Photocopiables

PAGE 28 Toys and games
28 Teacher's notes
30 Photocopiables

PAGE 40 Living things
40 Teacher's notes
42 Photocopiables

PAGE 52 Out and about
52 Teacher's notes
54 Photocopiables

Introduction

This book forms part of a new series of photocopiable activity books for the Early Years. The books and their accompanying CD-ROMs provide early years practitioners with a bank of lively, differentiated activities that focus on a particular skill or curriculum area. The chapters in each book are divided into popular themes.

The ideas in this book have been selected from previously published Scholastic early years series. They have been updated to meet new curriculum requirements and many have been differentiated, with alternative activity sheets for supporting and extending the work provided on the CD-ROM.

Using this book

Early Years Photocopiables – Communication, Language and Literacy contains five chapters based on the popular themes of 'Stories and rhymes'; 'Ourselves'; 'Toys and games'; 'Living things' and 'Out and about'. Each chapter contains two pages of teacher's notes and ten photocopiable activity sheets. The activities support work in the Communication, Language and Literacy Area of Learning and may be used in any order to suit your own planning.

The photocopiable activity sheets can be used in a flexible manner – you may wish to use some of the activities for assessment and record-keeping purposes and many are suitable for sending home with the children. This can be a useful method of ensuring a good dialogue with parents and carers, though it is necessary to be sensitive to issues that may arise as a result. Parents need to understand that the work is meant to be both fun and optional, and need to be helped to have a clear understanding of how to approach the learning with their child.

The Foundation Stage Curriculum

All the activities are linked directly to the Foundation Stage curriculum as set out by the QCA in its document, *Curriculum guidance for the foundation stage*. Each activity is based on one of the Early Learning Goals for Communication, Language and Literacy.

The teacher's notes

To maximise the potential of the activity sheets, it is important to use them in conjunction with the accompanying teacher's notes. The notes will not only explain the main use for each sheet, but often they provide suggestions for introducing, differentiating and reinforcing the concept. For those sheets that have differentiated versions supplied on the CD-ROM there are brief notes explaining how the sheets have been adapted in order to support and extend learning.

Using the photocopiable sheets

The photocopiable books are designed to be used in a number of ways. There may be suggestions in the teacher's notes to enlarge the sheet and copy it on to card or coloured paper. You may also choose to laminate some of the sheets, particularly those that will be used as games or for visual stimuli to promote discussion.

Many of the photocopiable sheets may be used several times, as they have been written as open-ended tasks and can be reapplied with a new theme or subject matter. For example, some of the sheets are designed to be used in role-play settings and provide templates for the children to use.

When using photocopiable activity sheets with early years children it is important that the work is set within a context. Spend some time introducing and explaining the work and be on hand to guide and support the children as they complete or record the activity.

The CD-ROM

The books in this series each have an accompanying CD-ROM containing the core activity sheets as featured in the book. These may be printed from your computer. In addition the CD-ROM contains an additional 60 activity sheets. These 60 printable sheets provide support and extension material for the core activities that they are linked to, enabling practitioners to plan and provide differentiated material to suit a broad range of stages and children's abilities.

The CD-ROM program should auto run when you insert the CD-ROM into your CD drive. If it does not, use 'My Computer' to browse the contents of the CD-ROM and click on the 'Early Years Photocopiables' icon. For further support in using the CD-ROM, click on the 'Help' notes on the 'Main menu' screen.

CHAPTER 1

Stories and rhymes

PAGE 6
Polly put the kettle on
Learning objective
Retell narratives in the correct sequence, drawing on language patterns of stories.

What to do
Teach the children the traditional rhyme, 'Polly put the kettle on'. Give each child a copy of the activity sheet and discuss the pictures. Can the children tell you which order the pictures should go in? Ask them to cut out the pictures and stick them on a piece of paper in the order of the rhyme.
Support: The pictures are numbered and the text is separated from the pictures.
Extension: There is space for the children to write two of the lines from the rhyme.

PAGE 7
The ugly duckling
Learning objective
Show an understanding of the elements of stories, such as main character, sequence of events, and openings, and how information can be found in non-fiction texts to answer questions about where, who, why and how.

What to do
Read or tell the children the traditional story of 'The Ugly Duckling'. Give each child a blank zig-zag book and the activity sheet. Read the story together again and discuss the pictures. Help the children to cut out and stick the pictures in the sequence of the story.
Support: The sequence is reduced to four pictures in simpler language.
Extension: There are four pictures with lines for the children to write their own version of the story.

PAGE 8
What's in a name?
Learning objective
Write their own names and other things such as labels and captions and begin to form some simple sentences, occasionally using punctuation.

What to do
Help the children to write their names on the book plates and colour in the pictures. Cut them out and stick them into favourite books or workbooks.

PAGE 9
Dear Teddy
Learning objective
Attempt writing for different purposes, using features of different forms such as lists, stories and instructions.

What to do
Talk about what things you might need for a picnic, such as the type of food and drink you may have. Ask the children to record their ideas in the space provided. Encourage them to have a go at writing some words, their names and any pictures. Share some published shape and novelty books and talk about what the children like about these kind of books.
Support: Dotted picnic words are provided for the children to trace.
Extension: Lines are provided for the children to write down words to match the pictures provided.

PAGE 10
Shape stories
Learning objective
Attempt writing for different purposes, using features of different forms such as lists, stories and instructions.

What to do
The activity sheet provides a template of a door with a lock for the children to cut out and fold to make a shape book. Use the shapes to inspire some imaginative stories. Ask the children to imagine they are going up the stairs and through a secret door. What

Stories and rhymes

lies behind the door? Help the children to write some words to tell their tale.

Goldilocks
PAGE 11

Listen with enjoyment, and respond to stories, songs and other music, rhymes and poems and make up their own stories, songs, rhymes and poems.

What to do
Use the pictures on the sheet to tell a version of the Goldilocks story. Now encourage the children to cut out the pictures and assemble them into a book (by sticking the pictures onto blank pages and stapling them together in the correct order). Ask them to tell the story to a partner.
Support: Just four pictures are provided for the children to put in the correct order.
Extension: Two pictures and four blank squares are provided for the children to add pictures or words.

Hey diddle diddle
PAGE 12

Learning objective
Listen with enjoyment, and respond to stories, songs and other music, rhymes and poems and make up their own stories, songs, rhymes and poems.

What to do
Read the nursery rhyme 'Hey diddle, diddle' to the children. Give each child a copy of the sheet and ask them to point to the characters as you say their names (there are extra characters to ensure that the children aren't simply guessing). Ask the children to colour in the pictures of those in the rhyme. Talk about the other characters and the rhymes they might appear in.

There was a crooked man
PAGE 13

Learning objective
Enjoy listening to and using spoken and written language, and readily turn to it in their play and learning.

What to do
Enjoy the traditional rhyme, 'There was a crooked man' together. Give each child a copy of the activity sheet and ask them to cut out the pictures, stick them onto card and fix a lolly stick or similar to each character card. Let them use the cards and pictures to retell the rhyme. Provide a story box to put the puppets, book and any other props into. Encourage the children to retell this rhyme (plus other favourites) when they have a spare moment.

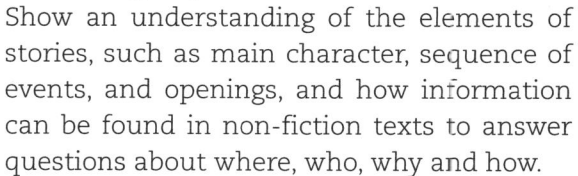

Humpty's fall
PAGE 14

Learning objective
Show an understanding of the elements of stories, such as main character, sequence of events, and openings, and how information can be found in non-fiction texts to answer questions about where, who, why and how.

What to do
Ask the children to tell you the traditional rhyme, 'Humpty Dumpty'. Talk about the characters in the story. Ask: *Who is the main character?* Give each child a copy of the activity sheet. Ask them to colour and cut out Humpty. Let them make a junk model wall and stick Humpty to it with sticky Velcro. Retell the rhyme, making Humpty fall off the wall at the appropriate point!

Colourful characters
PAGE 15

Learning objective
Listen with enjoyment, and respond to stories, songs and other music, rhymes and poems and make up their own stories, songs, rhymes and poems.

What to do
Look at the characters on the activity sheet. Ask the children if they remind them of any characters from stories or rhymes that they know. Give each child their own copy of the sheet and ask them to cut them out, stick them to card and attach sticks to make puppets. Let the children use them for some story-telling fun.

Name   Stories and rhymes

Polly put the kettle on

Polly put the kettle on,
We'll all have tea.

Polly put the kettle on,
Polly put the kettle on.

Sukey take it off again,
Sukey take it off again.

Sukey take it off again,
They've all gone away.

Name Stories and rhymes

The ugly duckling

All through the winter he hid in the bushes.

There were lots of yellow ducklings and one ugly duckling.

Once upon a time some eggs hatched in a duck's nest.

Then he saw some beautiful swans.

The swans said, 'You're a swan too'. The ugly duckling was very happy.

The other ducklings would not play with him.

What's in a name?

Stories and rhymes

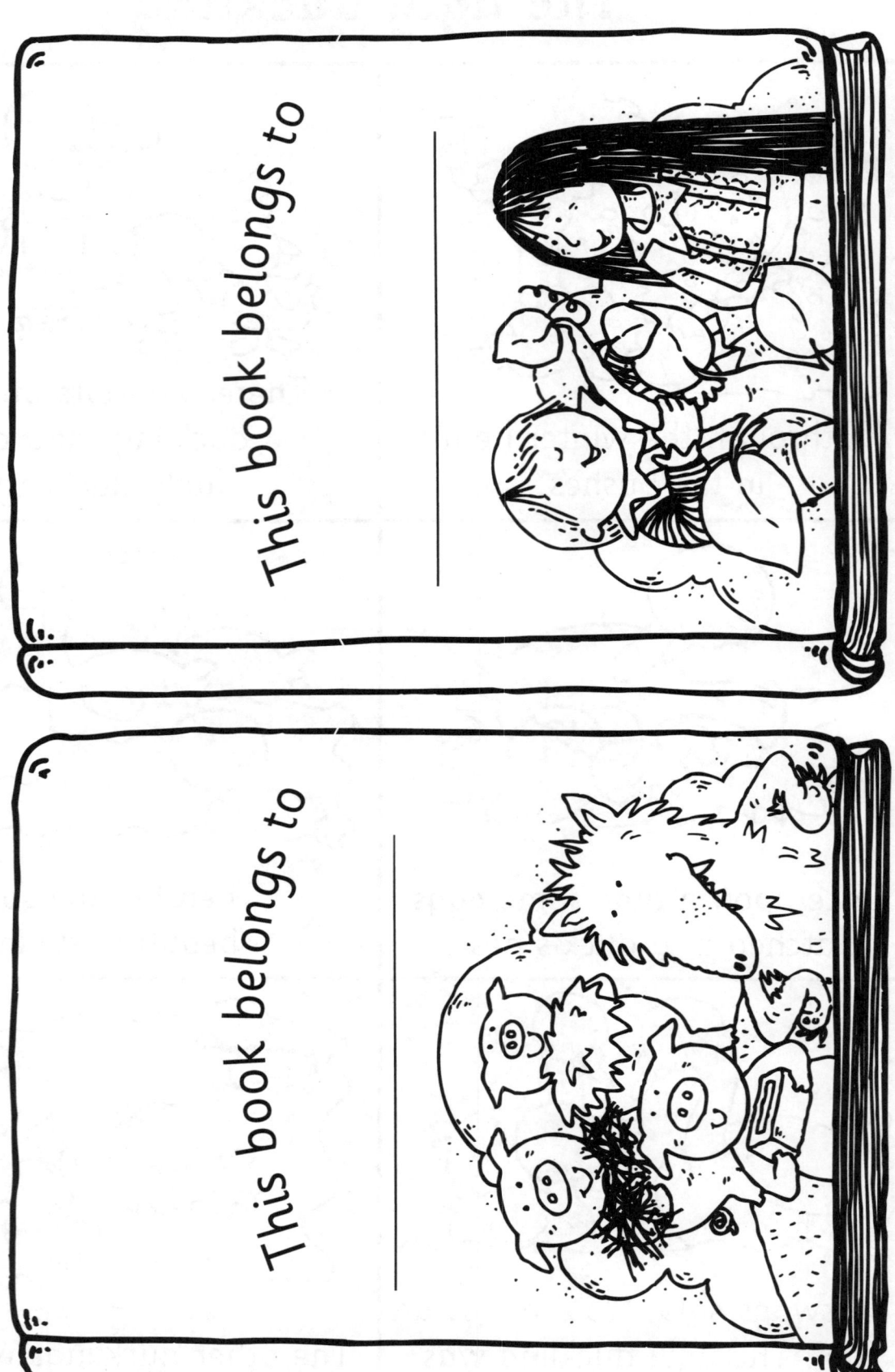

Name

Stories and rhymes

Dear Teddy

Dear Teddy

We are going to have a picnic.
Please bring

I hope you can come!

From

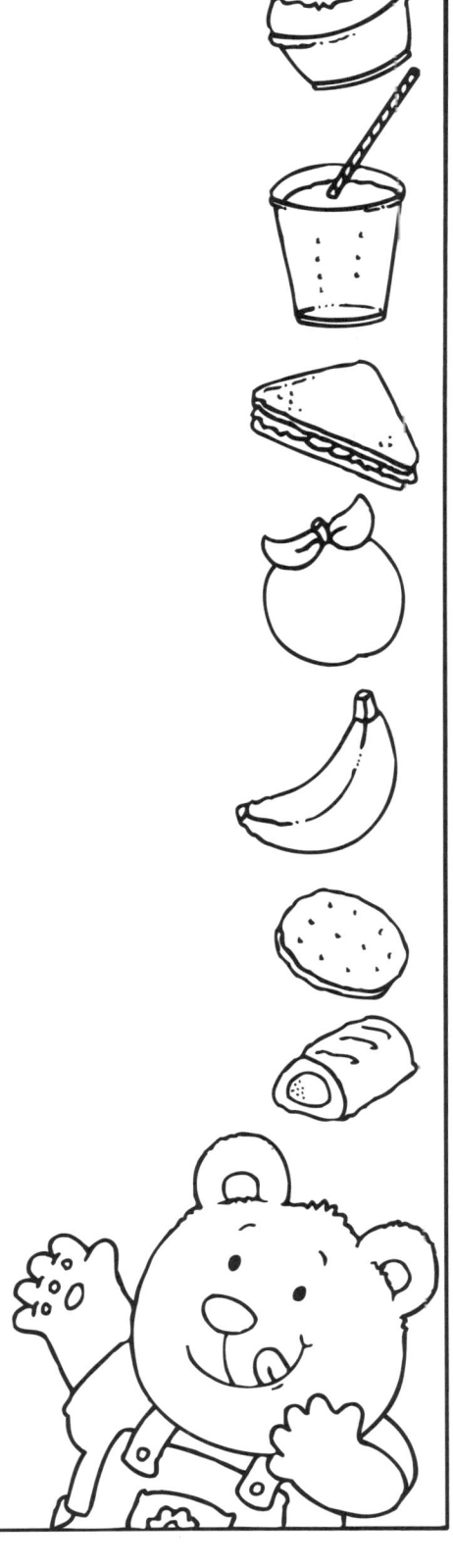

Name

Stories and rhymes

Shape stories

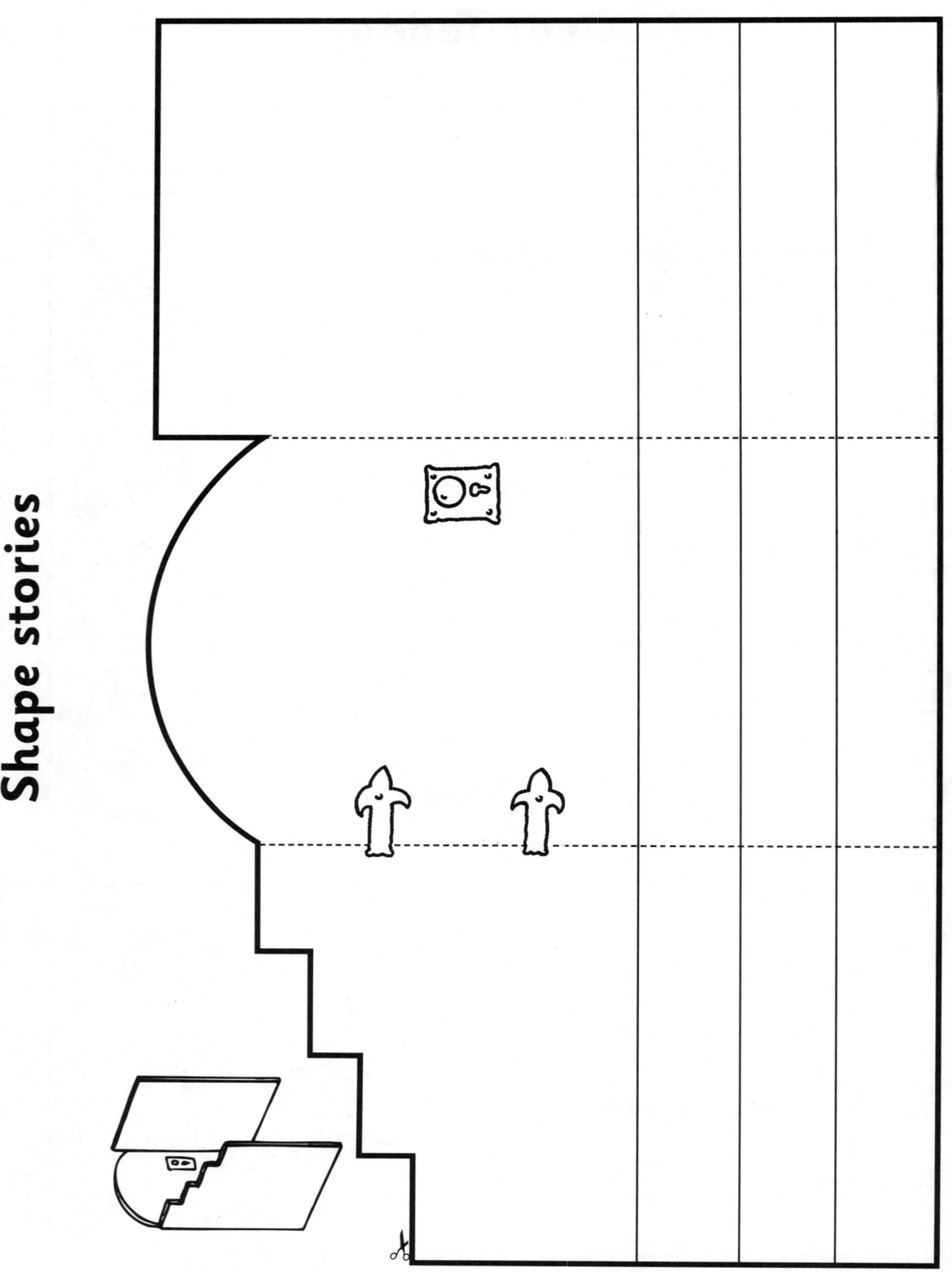

10 Communication, Language and Literacy

Stories and rhymes

Goldilocks

Hey diddle, diddle

Name | Stories and rhymes

There was a crooked man

Name — Stories and rhymes

Humpty's fall

Colour or paint Humpty and cut him out.

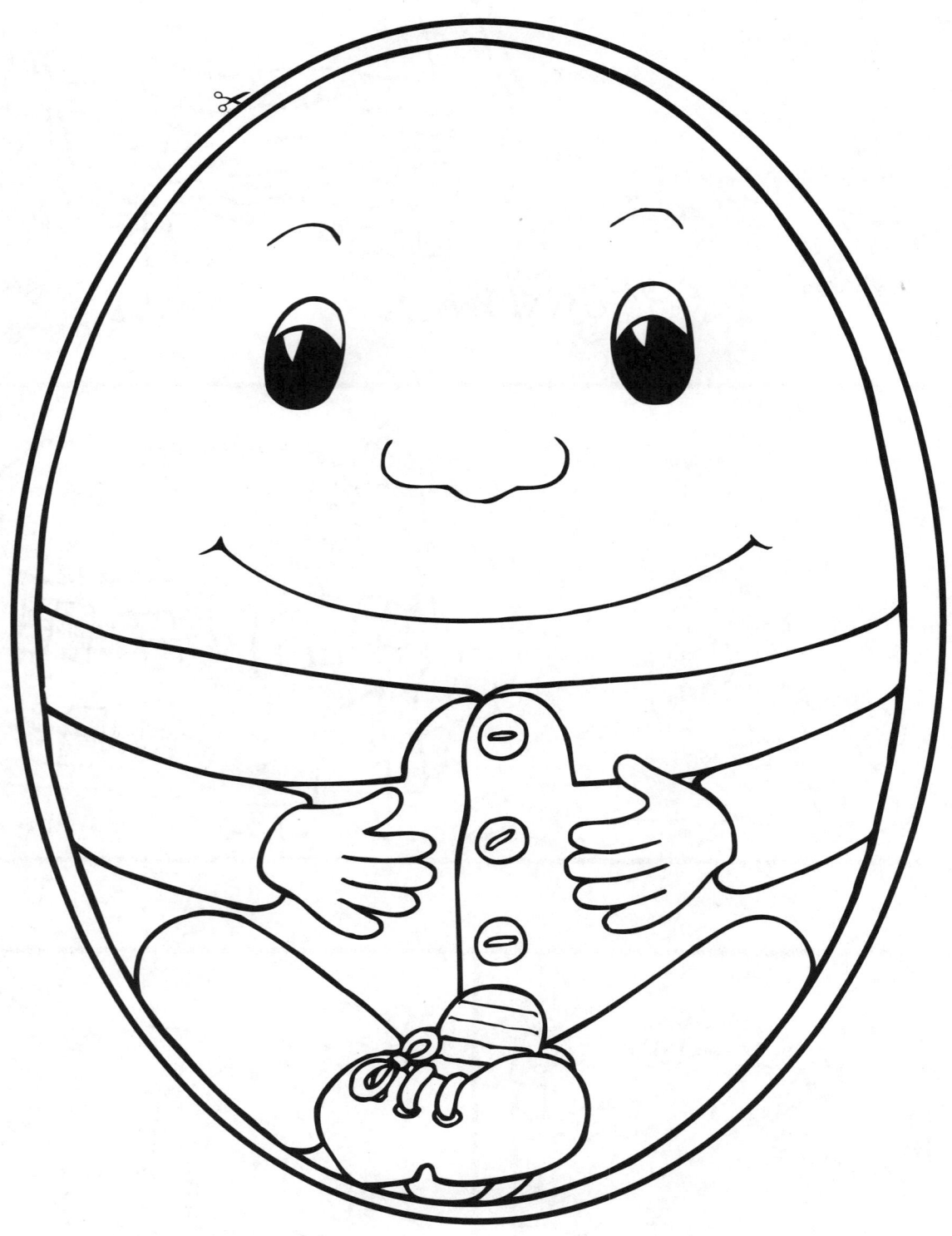

Name | Stories and rhymes

Colourful characters

Colour these in to make some characters for a play.

CHAPTER 2

Ourselves

PAGE 18 ### 'I can...' booklet

Learning objective
Write their own names and other things such as labels and captions and begin to form simple sentences, sometimes using punctuation.

What to do
Talk about all the things that the children are proud that they can do now that they are bigger. Give them a copy of the activity sheet and ask them to cut out the pictures and stick them onto pieces of paper to staple together to make a book. Ask the children to write their own names in the spaces provided. Add extra pages for the children to add further pictures and writing about the things they can do.

PAGE 19 ### 'I can...' booklet (2)

Learning objective
Write their own names and other things such as labels and captions and begin to form simple sentences, sometimes using punctuation.

What to do
Make the booklets, as in 'I can...' above. Challenge the children to think of some extra ideas for their books. Suggest that the children think about the pattern of a typical day to generate some ideas about the things that they can do. For example, they may be able to spread the butter on their own toast at breakfast time; do up their own coat; put on their own shoes and so on.

PAGE 20 ### All my own work

Learning objective
Write their own names and other things such as labels and captions and begin to form simple sentences, sometimes using punctuation.

What to do
Show the children some examples of name plates, book plates, name badges and so on. Provide each child with a copy of the sheet and ask them to write their name and colour in the picture to make their own special book or folder plates.

PAGE 21 ### Making it better

Learning objective
Use talk to organise, sequence and clarify thinking, ideas, feelings and events, thinking, ideas, feelings and events.

What to do
Enlarge a copy of the activity sheet and ask the children to describe what is happening in the pictures. Have the children ever experienced any of these situations at home or in the playground? Ask the children to consider what each of the children in the pictures might be thinking. Are they angry or sad? What might happen next to make everything better again?
Support: There are two larger pictures provided to talk about with the children.
Extension: The same two pictures that are used for the less able children are provided, this time with space for the children to write underneath.

PAGE 22 ### Baby care

Learning objective
Use talk to organise, sequence and clarify thinking, ideas, feelings and events.

What to do
Show the children an enlarged copy of the activity sheet. Talk about all the things that a baby needs, explaining that some can be seen such as a cot and others can't be seen such as warmth and love. Encourage the children to add ideas of their own as well as the things that they can see.

Ourselves

Support: Specific word examples are given for the children to find in the picture and discuss.

Extension: The children must find some examples of objects on the activity sheet. There are lines provided for the children to write some of the words. Discuss with the children the various objects they have found.

PAGE 23

Happy memories

Learning objective
Use language to imagine and recreate roles and experiences.

What to do
Provide each child with a copy of the activity sheet to take home. Encourage the children's families to talk with them about happy memories and to help them to fill in the sheets to bring back and share with the rest of the group.

PAGE 24

All about me

Learning objective
Use language to imagine and recreate roles and experiences.

What to do
Talk to the children about when they were babies. Do they ever look at baby photographs at home? Have they been told any funny stories about the things they used to do? Now remind them of the things they could and couldn't do as toddlers, such as put their socks and shoes on, or use a knife and fork. Now ask them to think about something they did yesterday. Work with individuals and scribe a line or two using their own words. Use the opportunity to introduce and reinforce the vocabulary associated with time, using words such as 'before', 'yesterday' and so on.

Support: There are dotted words for the children to trace over.

Extension: The last picture has been left blank for the children to draw a full-length picture of themselves.

PAGE 25

Whatever next?

Learning objective
Use talk to organise, sequence and clarify thinking, ideas, feelings and events.

What to do
Give each child a copy of the sheet and encourage them to talk about the pictures, relating them to their own experiences. Invite them to think up a happy ending for each one and discuss these ideas with the whole group.

PAGE 26

Perfecting the process

Learning objective
Write their own names and other things such as labels and captions and begin to form simple sentences, sometimes using punctuation.

What to do
The activity sheet shows a number of keys from a keyboard (assuming that the keyboard has been covered with lower case letter stickers). Encourage the children to press the keys in the correct order to make the words 'my name is'. Ask the children to key in their own name after the phrase.

PAGE 27

Things we do

Learning objective
Interact with others, negotiating plans and activities and taking turns in conversation.

What to do
Work with small groups of children. Talk together about what the children can see in the activity pictures. Ask them, in turn, to talk about experiences they have had that relate to one of the pictures. Encourage the children to take turns and to listen to each other.

Support: The activity is reduced to four pictures to talk about.

Extension: Three spaces are provided for the children to draw some of the everyday things that they do.

Ourselves

I can... booklet (2)

Make these pictures into a book.

I can ——————

I can roll

—————————————

I can ——————

I can skip

Boys make good pets, everyone should own one.

Name Ourselves

All my own work

This belongs to _____

Communication, Language and Literacy

Name

Ourselves

Making it better

What is happening and how could we make it better?

Name | Ourselves

Baby care

What things does a new baby need?

Name   Ourselves

Happy memories

Talk with your family about the happiest things you can remember. Ask them to write them down using your words. Do you have a photograph you can bring in to share?

The three most wonderful things that ever happened to me were…

1. When _____

_____

_____

2. When _____

_____

_____

3. When _____

_____

_____

How did they make you feel?

Name

Ourselves

All about me

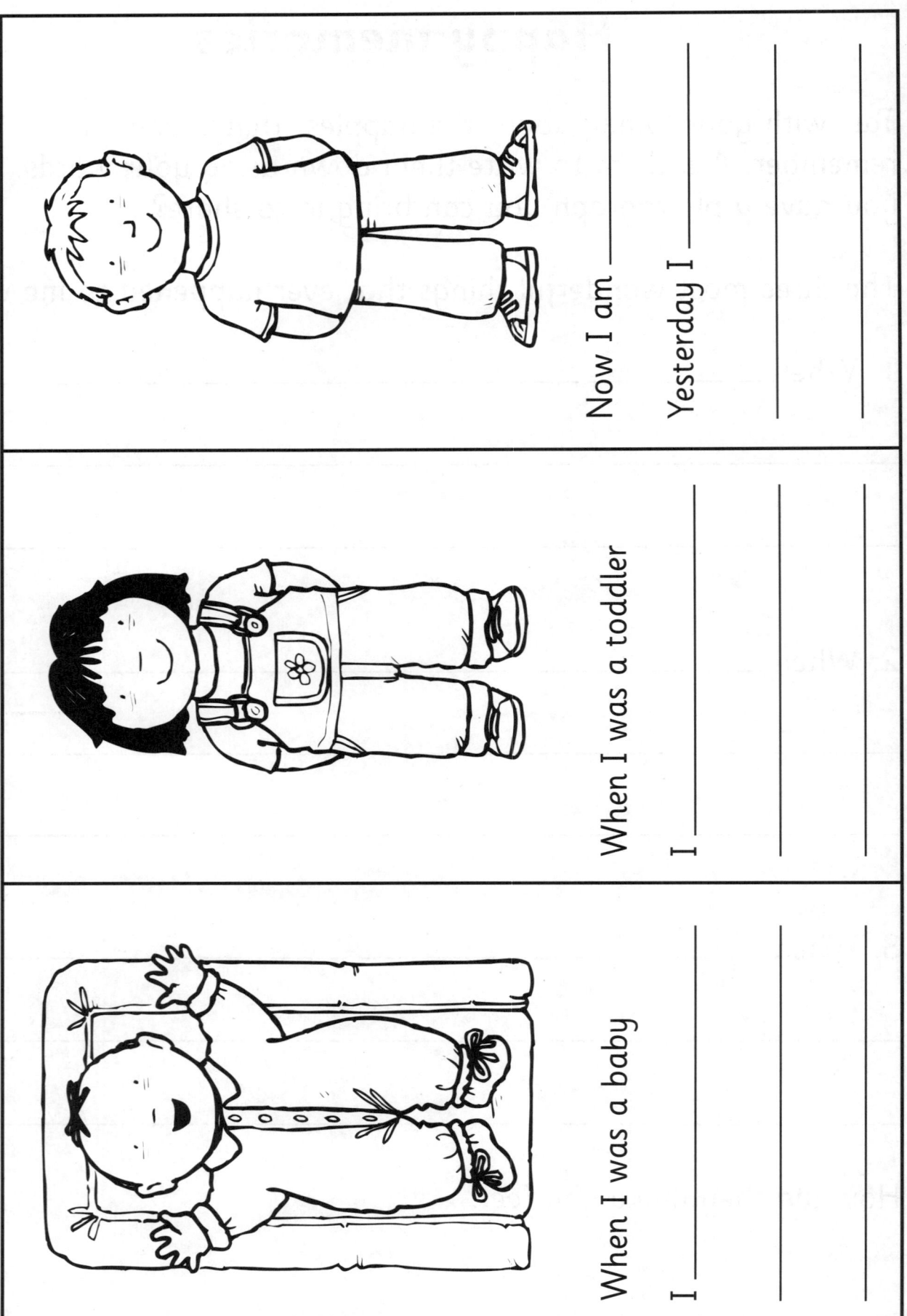

Now I am _____
Yesterday I _____
_____

When I was a toddler _____
I _____
_____

When I was a baby _____
I _____
_____

Name | Ourselves

Whatever next?

Name

Ourselves

Perfecting the process

Press these keys in this order.

On your screen you should have: my name is

Can you key in your name now?

Communication, Language and Literacy

Things we do

Talk about what is happening in the pictures.

CHAPTER 3

Toys and games

PAGE 30 Two's company

Learning objective
Use language to imagine and recreate roles and experiences.

What to do
Use the activity sheet as a talking point to discuss which games and toys are more fun when played with someone else. Ask the children to share their experiences of games that they have shared with someone that would not have been much fun if they had played them by themselves.
Support: Five pictures only to discuss.
Extension: Space for the children to write about their favourite game.

PAGE 31 Show and tell

Learning objective
Attempt writing for different purposes, using features of different forms such as lists, stories and instructions.

What to do
Talk about what Teddy is doing in each picture on the sheet. Give each child their own sheet and ask them to draw a picture of Teddy doing something else. Encourage them to 'have-a-go' at writing down the words.
Support: The final box has a caption supplied for children to illustrate.
Extension: There is space under each picture for the children to write.

PAGE 32 Formula one

Learning objective
Use a pencil and hold it effectively to form recognisable letters, most of which are correctly formed.

What to do
Talk about the racing tracks on the activity sheet. Ask the children to have a go at tracing each track carefully, first with a finger, and then with a pencil. Encourage them to concentrate on keeping their car on the track!
Support: Three simple tracks to follow.
Extension: More demanding tracks plus letter formation practice.

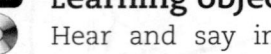

PAGE 33 Katie's kite

Learning objective
Hear and say initial and final sounds in words, and short vowel sounds within words.

What to do
Give each child a copy of the sheet. Explain that the children on the sheet are called Katie and Mohammed. Katie is collecting all the 'k' things and Mohammed is collecting all the 'm' things. Ask the children to draw lines to join the children to the matching objects. Continue the activity by suggesting that the children look for three or four things that begin with the same letter as their own name.
Support: Only four pictures to match, plus the characters are wearing their letters on their shirts.
Extension: The children must write the correct letters in the boxes next to each item/character.

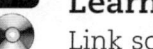

PAGE 34 Letter games

Learning objective
Link sounds to letters, naming and sounding the letters of the alphabet.

What to do
Before you begin to play the game, check that the children recognise all the letters on the game board and that they know what the pictures represent. Use counters and a dice numbered (0-2) to play the game with pairs of children. Provide each child with a counter and ask them to take turns to move around

Toys and games

the board, landing on the letters and pictures. Before they can move on they must think of an object beginning with that letter or a word to rhyme with the picture.
Support: There are less letters as the focus in this activity and only two rhyming pictures.
Extension: Some of the squares have two letters. There is an extra picture for rhyming work.

Happy families
Learning objective
Hear and say initial and final sounds in words and short vowel sounds within words.

What to do
Copy the activity sheet onto card. Ask each child to colour the pictures and cut out the jigsaw pieces. Can they make the jigsaw words?
Support: The pieces are matched opposite each other on the sheet. Mini versions of the pictures help matching skills.
Extension: The children need to work out the picture to draw on the blank piece of puzzle. they also have to write the initial letters in the spaces.

My colourful monster
Learning objective
Read a range of familiar and common words and simple sentences independently.

What to do
Give each child a copy of the sheet. Encourage them to read the colour words and decorate the monster accordingly.
Support: Boxes are provided for the practitioner to colour appropriately to help the children.
Extension: Extra labels are provided for the children to read and complete.

Tell the story
Learning objective
Retell narratives in the correct sequence, drawing on language patterns of stories.

What to do
Give each child in a small group a copy of the activity sheet. Discuss the pictures and the sequence of events. Encourage the children to use story language as they tell the story to you. Let the children cut out the pictures then reassemble them in the correct order in a zig-zag book or on paper.
Support: The activity has only four pictures to sequence.
Extension: There are four pictures plus two blank boxes for the children to draw their own pictures to conclude the story.

Playtime
Learning objective
Use a pencil and hold it effectively to form recognisable letters, most of which are correctly formed.

What to do
Give each child a copy of the sheet and ask them to imagine where they think the missing balls might be. The children need to form circle shapes. Talk about letters that use 'circle' or round shapes. Identify them on an alphabet chart.
Support: There are four pictures only for this activity.
Extension: In addition to drawing in where they think the balls should be there is some letter formation practice.

Follow the path
Learning objective
Use a pencil and hold it effectively to form recognisable letters, most of which are correctly formed.

What to do
Give each child a copy of the activity sheet and explain that you would like them to use a pencil to trace over the route from the bear to the honey pot.
Support: In this activity there are no obstacles to pass.
Extension: The children have to draw their own route around the obstacles.

Name   Toys and games

Two's company

Which toys do you play with on your own?
Which are more fun if you play with someone else?

Name Toys and games

Show and tell

Teddy is hiding.

Teddy is getting ready for bed.

Teddy is sharing his sweets.

Name

Toys and games

Formula one

32 Communication, Language and Literacy

Name | Toys and games

Katie's kite

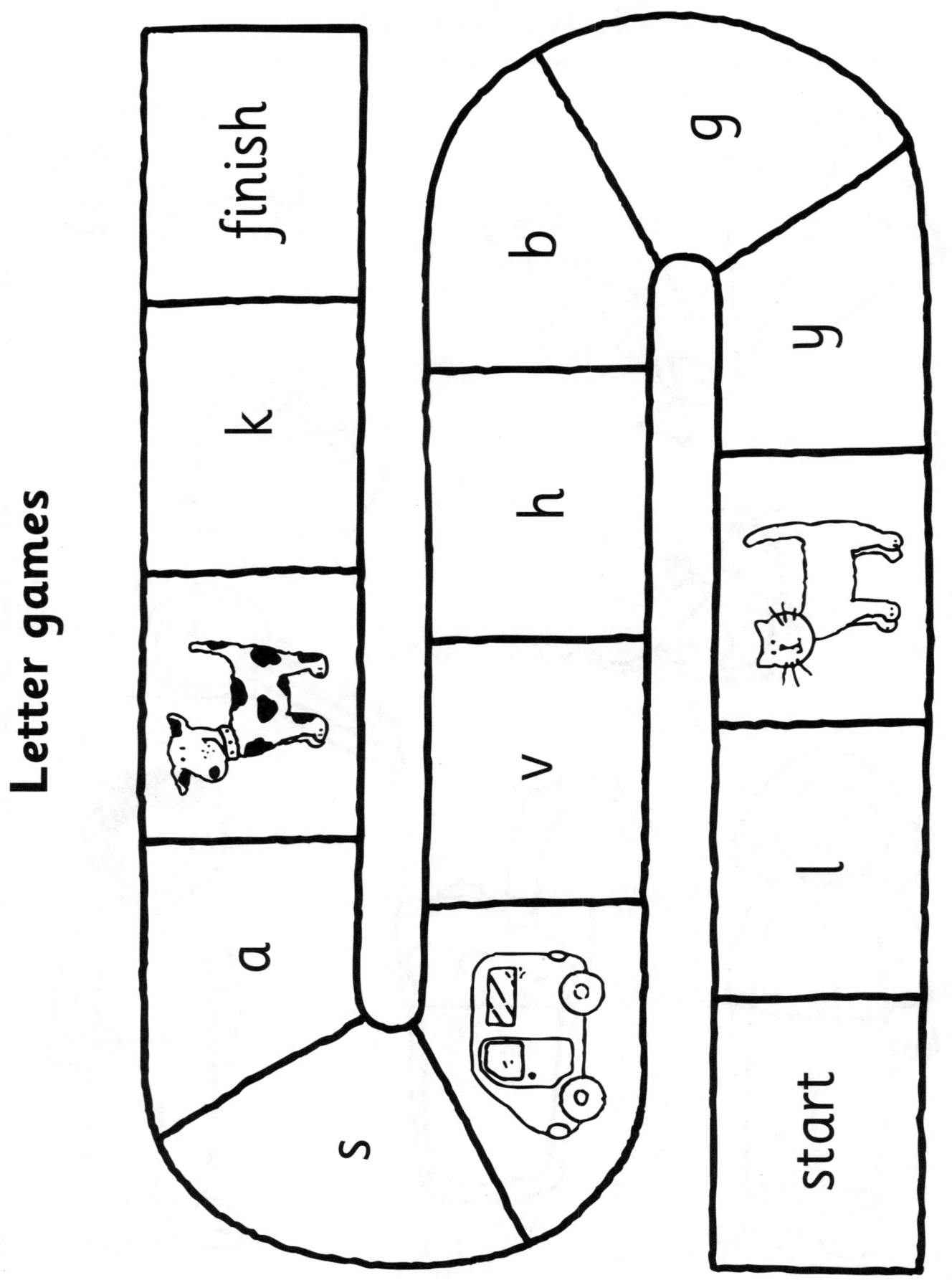

Happy families

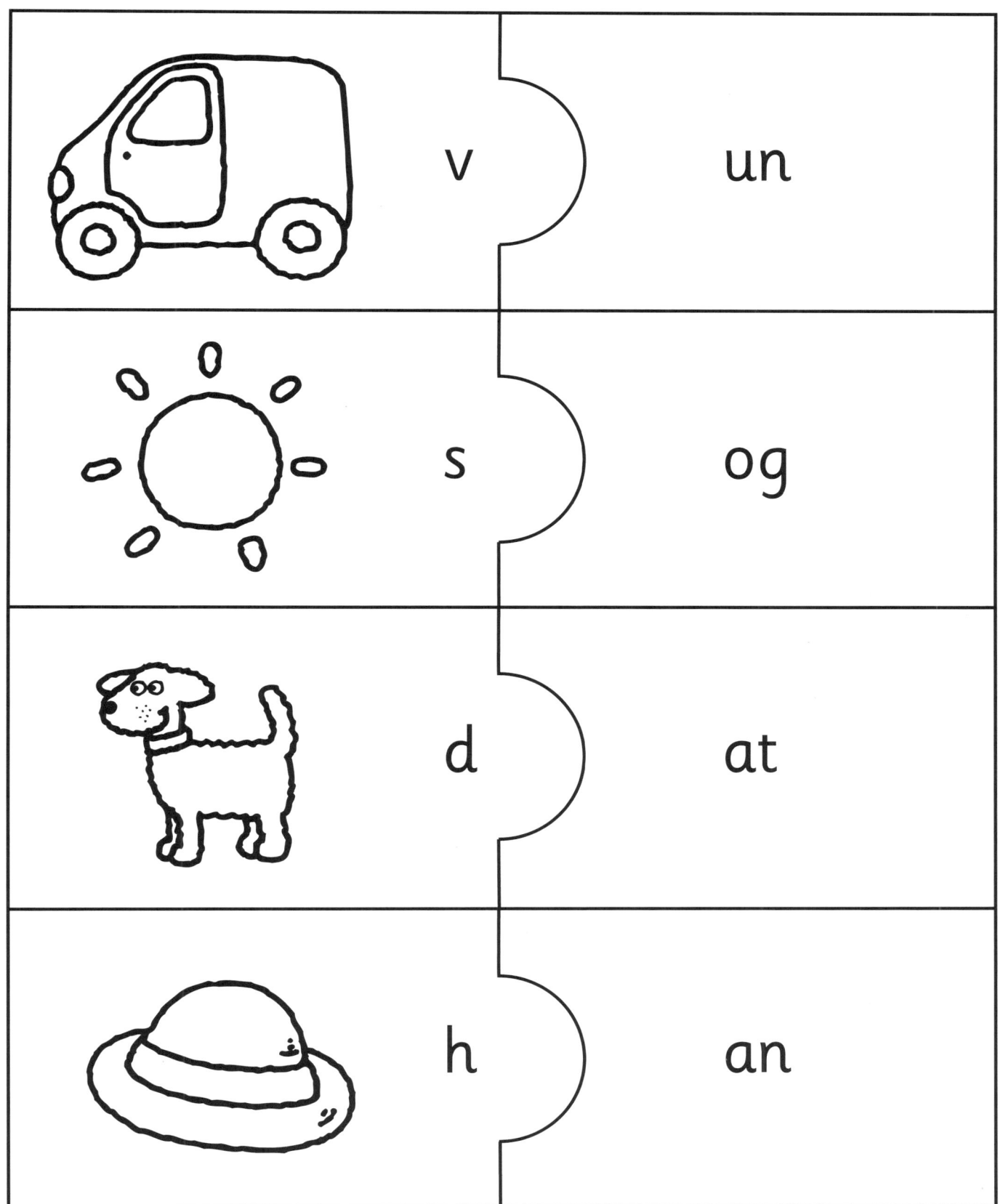

Name | Toys and games

My colourful monster

Name

Toys and games

Tell the story

Cut out the pictures and tell the story.

Name

Toys and games

Playtime

The children are playing. Draw five balls.

Name

Toys and games

Follow the path

Help the bear to get to the honey.

CHAPTER 4
Living things

Make a mark
PAGE 42

Learning objective
Use a pencil and hold it effectively to form recognisable letters, most of which are correctly formed.

What to do
Provide a range of types of colouring tools, such as pencils, crayons and pastels. Encourage the children to experiment with making marks of different size, shape and pressure to fill the cat's tummy!
Support: There are dotted line patterns for the children to trace over.
Extension: The cat's tummy is filled with the letters 'c', 'a' and 't' for the children to trace over and then write for themselves.

Tongue twisting
PAGE 43

Learning objective
Hear and say initial and final sounds in words, and short vowel sounds within words.

What to do
Tell the children a tongue-twisting rhyme such as 'Peter Piper picked a peck of pickled peppers'. Ask the children what letter sound they can hear at the start of most of the words. Help the children to make glove puppets by cutting out the shapes, folding along the centre lines and taping the sides together. Ask the children to make up alliterative names for their puppets such as Lucy Ladybird or Benjamin Butterfly!

Multicoloured cat
PAGE 44

Learning objective
Link sounds to letters, naming and sounding the letters of the alphabet.

What to do
Encourage the children to match colours to the letter sounds on the sheet, such as 'g' for 'green' and 'b' for 'blue'. Ask them to colour the cat using colours that correspond to the letters.
Support: The children are asked to match just two letters/colours.
Extension: The children are asked to fill in the missing letters of some colour words.

Make a rhyme
PAGE 45

Learning objective
Use their phonic knowledge to write simple regular words and make phonetically plausible attempts at more complex words.

What to do
Introduce the activity by discussing words that rhyme in the '-at' family. Ask the children to think of as many as possible. Discuss the examples on the photocopiable sheet and ask the children to complete the missing words and draw corresponding pictures.
Support: The children can trace over the dotted missing letters.
Extension: The children must supply the missing letters from the word 'cat' as well 'hat' and 'mat'.

Flap book
PAGE 46

Learning objective
Attempt writing for different purposes, using features of different forms such as lists, stories and instructions.

What to do
Discuss creatures that live in ponds and rivers. Explain that you would like the children to complete the activity sheet by continuing the theme, adding three, then four creatures to create a counting lift-the-flap book.
Support: There are pictures provided for each page of the book.
Extension: There is space for the children to write one or two words for each page.

Living things

PAGE 47 — The colourful caterpillar

Learning objective
Use a pencil and hold it effectively to form recognisable letters, most of which are correctly formed.

What to do
Ask the children to print different types of mark or pattern in each segment of the caterpillar. Let them use different mark-making tools to suit their stage of development.

PAGE 48 — Flower circles

Learning objective
Use a pencil and hold it effectively to form recognisable letters, most of which are correctly formed.

What to do
Ask the children to practise drawing circle shapes in the air with their fingers. Look together at an alphabet frieze. What letters have circle shapes in them? Ask the children to complete the flower by tracing over the dotted circles.
Support: The activity sheet provides some circles already complete, one half-finished and two dotted.
Extension: There are a variety of different sized circles for the children to complete. There is also a stalk to complete.

PAGE 49 — Planting and growing

Learning objective
Show an understanding of the elements of stories, such as main character, sequence of events, and openings, and how information can be found in non-fiction texts to answer questions about where, who, why and how.

What to do
Let each child plant their own seed or bean using the pictures in the activity sheet as a guide. Talk about the sequence of events together. Now give each child an activity sheet and ask them to cut out and sequence the pictures, turning them into a mini book.
Support: There are just four pictures for the children to cut out and sequence. There is some accompanying text for the practitioner to read out.
Extension: This activity has four pictures to sequence with space for writing underneath each one.

PAGE 50 — A patterned fish

Learning objective
Use a pencil and hold it effectively to form recognisable letters, most of which are correctly formed.

What to do
Talk about straight and curved letters and patterns with the children. Ask the children to show you examples of straight and curvy letters, patterns and objects from around the room. Help the children to finish the patterns on the activity sheet using bright colours.
Support: Dotted patterns are provided all the way across the fish for the children to trace over.
Extension: The children are asked to write some curved and straight letters in the space provided.

PAGE 51 — Chick, chick, chicken

Learning objective
Show an understanding of the elements of stories, such as main character, sequence of events, and openings, and how information can be found in non-fiction texts to answer questions about where, who, why and how.

What to do
Look at the pictures on the activity sheet together and discuss what they show. Ask the children to decide whether the pictures are in the correct order. Invite them to cut out the pictures, order them correctly and then paste them onto a separate piece of paper.
Support: The pictures are numbered and in the right order on the sheet.
Extension: The children are required to add two extra pictures to the sequence.

Name | Living things

Make a mark

42 Communication, Language and Literacy

Name

Living things

Tongue twisting

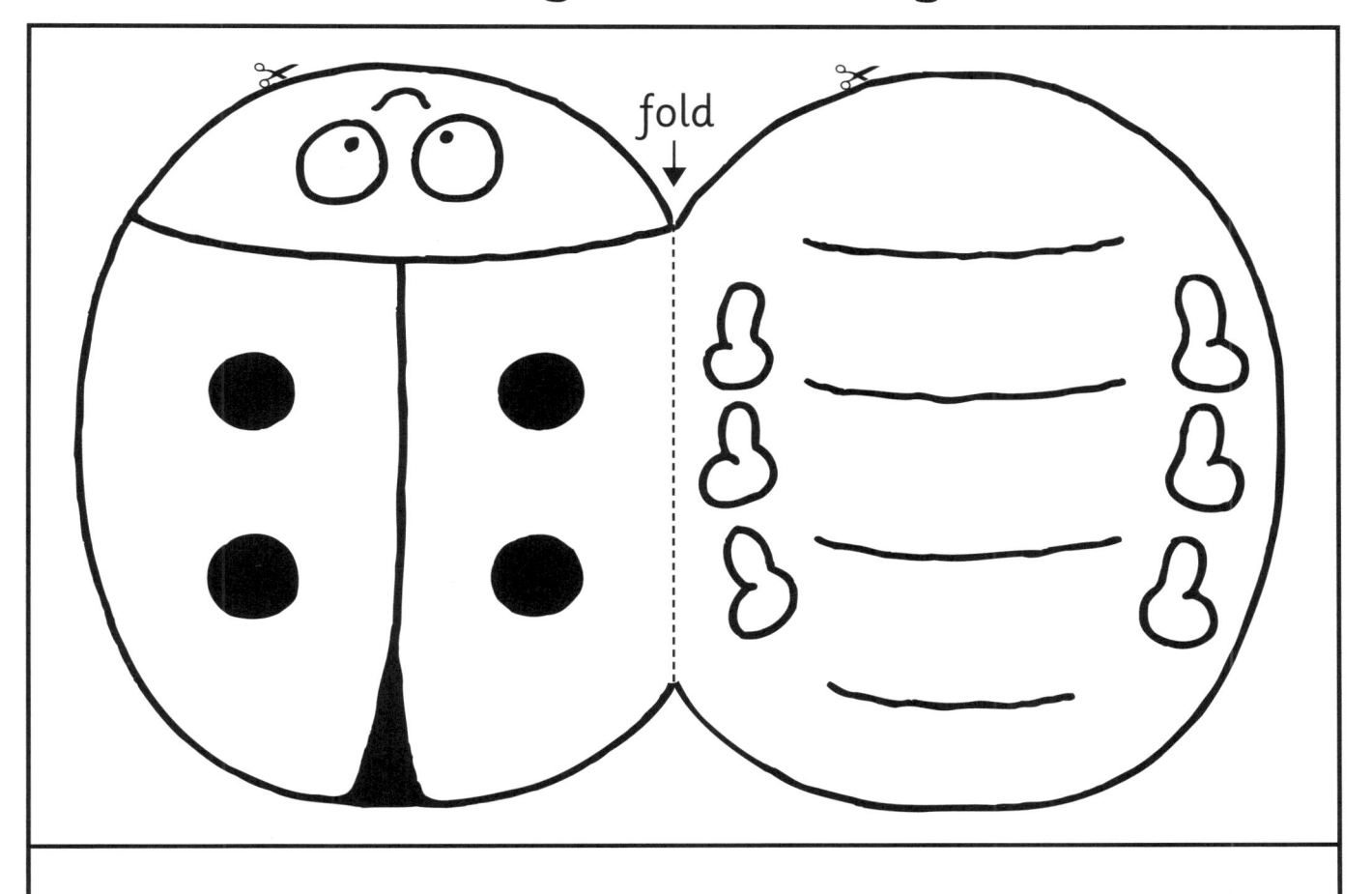

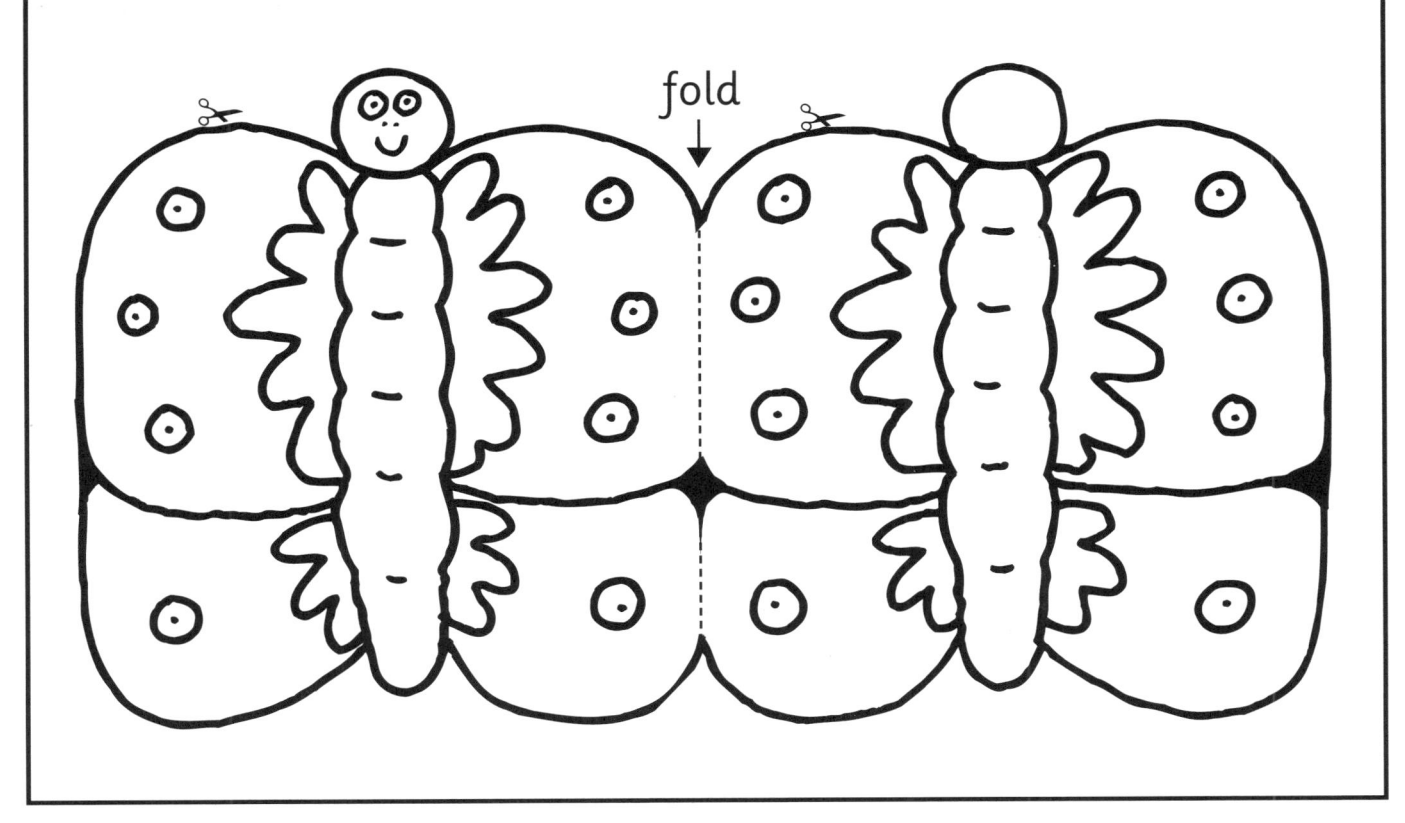

fold

fold

Name | Living things

Multicoloured cat

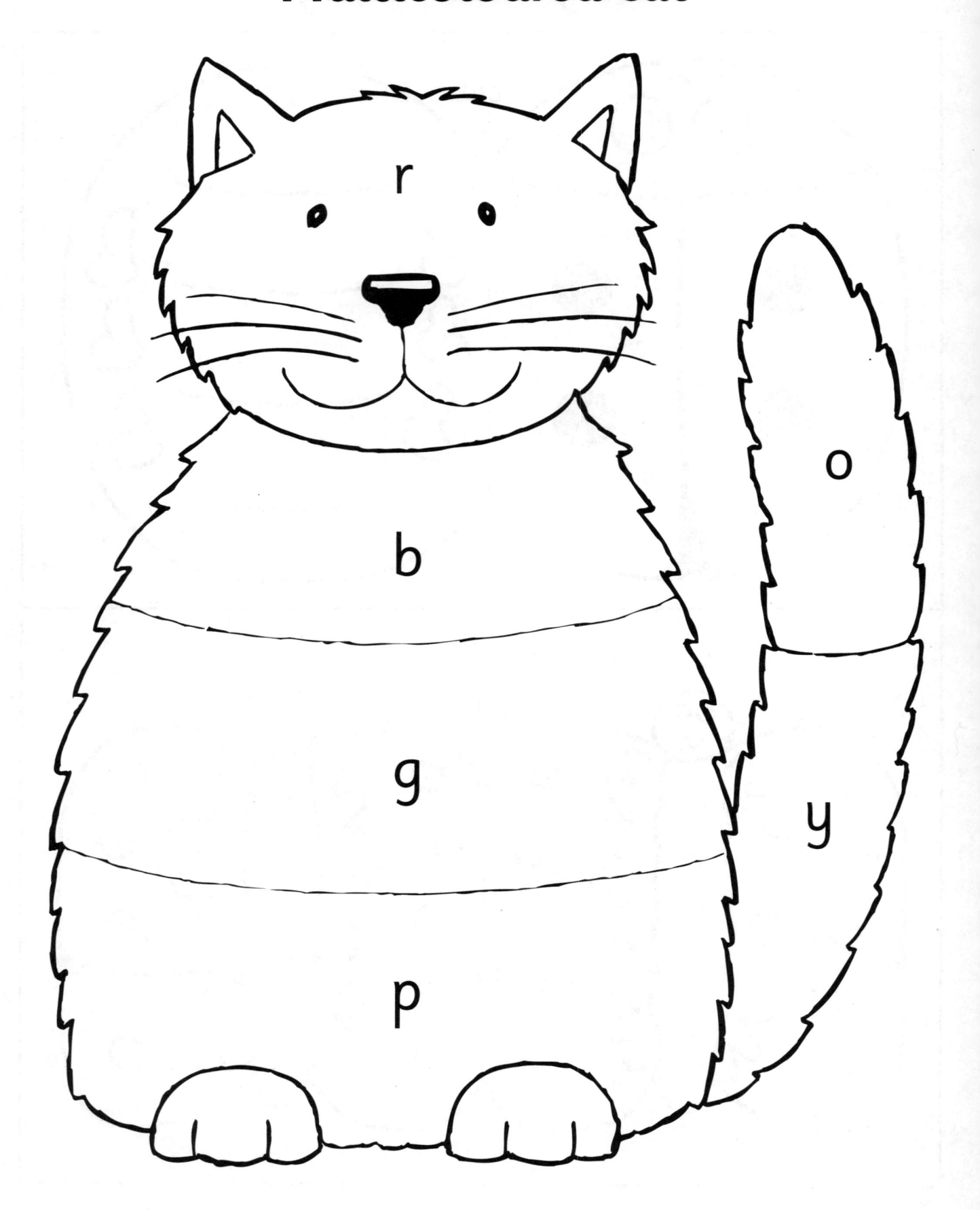

r

b

g

p

o

y

Name

Living things

Make a rhyme

Fill in the missing letters and draw the pictures.

cat
hat
mat

h __ __

m __ __

cat

Name | Living things

Flap book

Draw two more pictures and make your own flap book.

fold

Name

Living things

The colourful caterpillar

Print some patterns on the caterpillar.

Name | Living things

Flower circles

Place your pencil on each dot.
Draw a circle by following the arrow.
Colour in your flower picture.

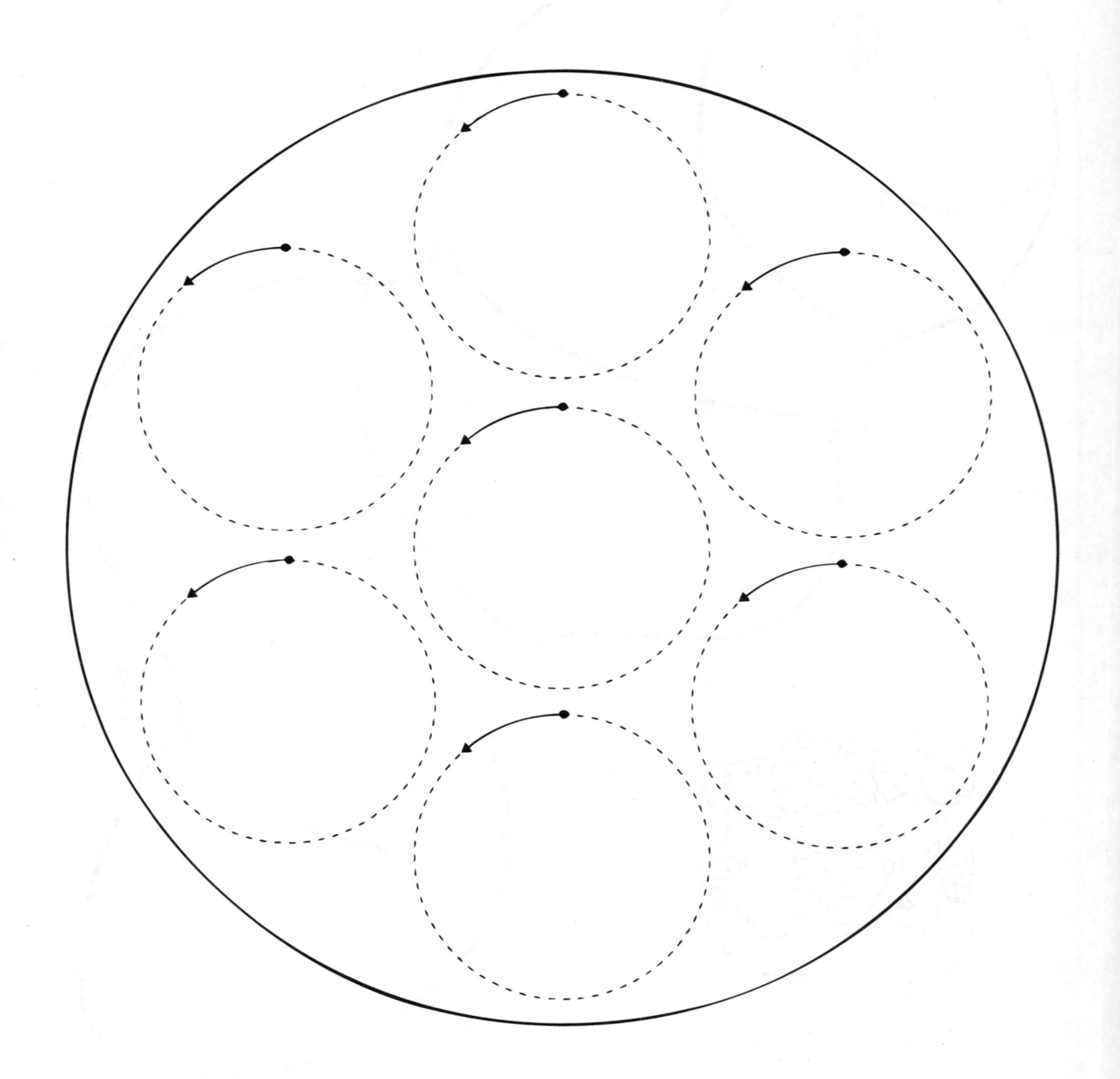

Name

Living things

Planting and growing

Colour in and cut out the pictures, and put them in order.

By _____

A patterned fish

Finish these patterns and bubbles with bright colours.

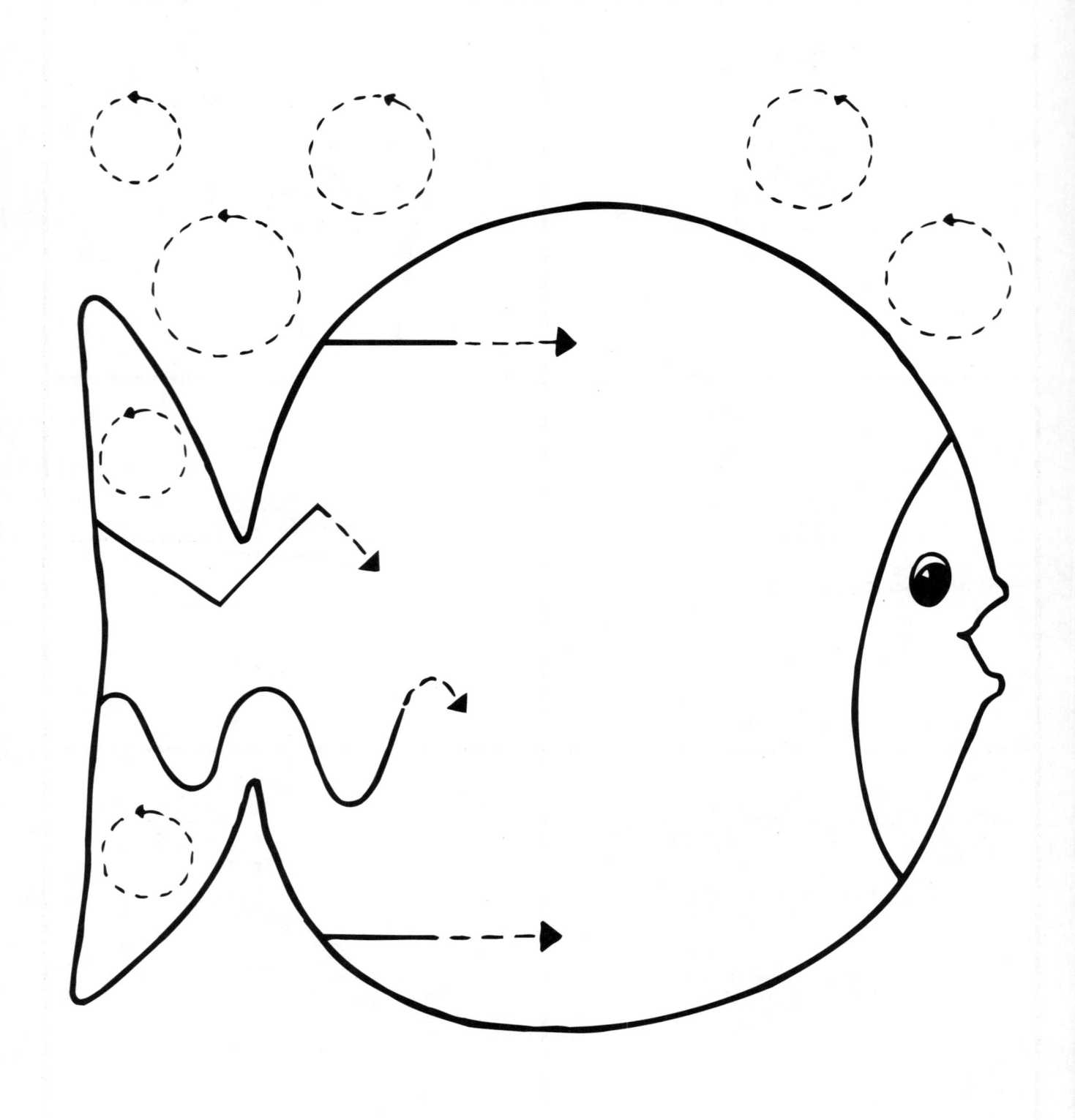

Name | Living things

Chick, chick, chicken

CHAPTER 5

Out and about

Going shopping
PAGE 54

Learning objective
Retell narratives in the correct sequence, drawing on language patterns of stories.

What to do
Talk about the children's experiences of going shopping. Give each child a copy of the activity sheet and explain that the pictures are muddled up and need to be put in the right order. Let them cut out and then paste the pictures in order on a piece of card that can be folded to create a zig-zag book.

At the seaside
PAGE 55

Learning objective
Hear and say initial and final sounds in words, and short vowel sounds within words.

What to do
Give each child a copy of the photocopiable sheet. Explain that the seaside picture contains a lot of words that begin with the letter 's'. How many 's' seaside words can the children think of? Are they all on the picture? Are there any on the picture that they hadn't thought of? Ask the children to find and circle all the 's' words at the seaside before colouring the picture.
Support: There are a list of 's' words provided for the practitioner to read out to the children.
Extension: A box is provided for the children to write a list of 's' words into.

Sort the shopping
PAGE 56

Learning objective
Link sounds to letters, naming and sounding the letters of the alphabet.

What to do
Bring in a bag full of shopping to play a game with the children. Ask them to guess what is in your shopping bag by giving them some clues, including the letter sound that the object starts with. For example: 'I begin with the letter 'a'. I am round and green and red. I am a crunchy, delicious fruit. What am I?'
Give each child a copy of the activity sheet. Explain that the shopping needs to be sorted out. Ask them to cut out the items and put them in the bag with the matching letter.
Support: The children concentrate on the two letters, 'c' and 'j'.
Extension: There are three blank spaces for the children to add their own examples.

Shopping day
PAGE 57

Learning objective
Extend their vocabulary, exploring the meanings and sounds of new words.

What to do
Enlarge the photocopiable sheet to A3 size and work with small groups of children at a time. Talk about the busy scene together, encouraging the children to use the relevant vocabulary, introducing new words as appropriate. Invite the children to talk about their own shopping experiences.

Make a story
PAGE 58

Learning objective
Enjoy listening to and using spoken and written language, and readily turn to it in their play and learning.

What to do
Enlarge the activity sheet to A3 size and work with small groups. Let the children take it in turns to choose a set of pictures to describe. Can they think of a different story to the previous speaker? Make sure that the children listen attentively to each other's stories. Check the children's understanding by asking them to ask each other questions about each of their stories.

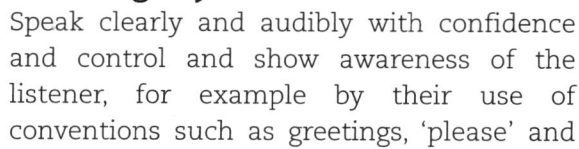

Out and about

Support: Two sets of pictures only are provided.
Extension: Two sets of pictures are provided with lines under each set for the children to write on.

PAGE 59 — A busy park

Learning objective
Speak clearly and audibly with confidence and control and show awareness of the listener, for example by their use of conventions such as greetings, 'please' and 'thank you'.

What to do
Enlarge the photocopiable sheet to at least A3 size and display it so that a large group of children can see it clearly. Invite the children to take it in turns to tell the rest of the group about something that interests them in the picture, perhaps they can relate it to an experience they had when they have been out with their own families. Encourage each speaker to say something different – this will encourage good listening as well as speaking skills.

PAGE 60 — Listening lotto

Learning objective
Sustain attentive listening, responding to what they have heard by relevant comments, questions or actions.

What to do
Make a recording of all the sounds shown on the activity sheet. Sit groups of up to six children around a table in a quiet space. Provide each child with six counters and a copy of the sheet. Play back the recordings you have made, asking the children to cover the pictures as they hear the matching sounds.

PAGE 61 — Praying together

Learning objective
Use language to imagine and recreate roles and experiences.

What to do
Enlarge a copy of the activity sheet to A3 size and use it to promote a discussion about praying, celebrating and being with our families. Encourage individuals to tell the rest of the group about their own experiences of prayer or other things that they do with their families. Talk about events, such as festivals, that the children have shared with each other as a group.

PAGE 62 — Garages

Learning objective
Attempt writing for different purposes, using features of different forms such as lists, stories and instructions.

What to do
Set up your role-play or outdoor area as a garage. Provide tools, large wheeled vehicles, overalls and copies of the activity sheet fixed to clipboards. Talk about MOTs and having a car serviced with the children and find out if they know what a registration number is. Ask the children if they know the various parts of a car, such as the boot, steering wheel and engine. Play alongside the children and help them to use the forms as part of their garage role-play.

PAGE 63 — A sailor went to sea

Learning objective
Use a pencil and hold it effectively to form recognisable letters, most of which are correctly formed.

What to do
Provide each child with a copy of the sheet and a sharp pencil. Encourage them to follow the 'waves' carefully, in the direction of the arrows. Talk about any wavy letters that the children know. Practise drawing wavy shapes and wavy letters in the air with fingers.
Support: The top dotted line is solid in each example.
Extension: The children are asked to practise writing the 'wavy' letters: 'w' and 'm' on the activity sheet.

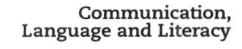

Going shopping

Cut out the pictures and put them in the right order.

Name

Out and about

At the seaside

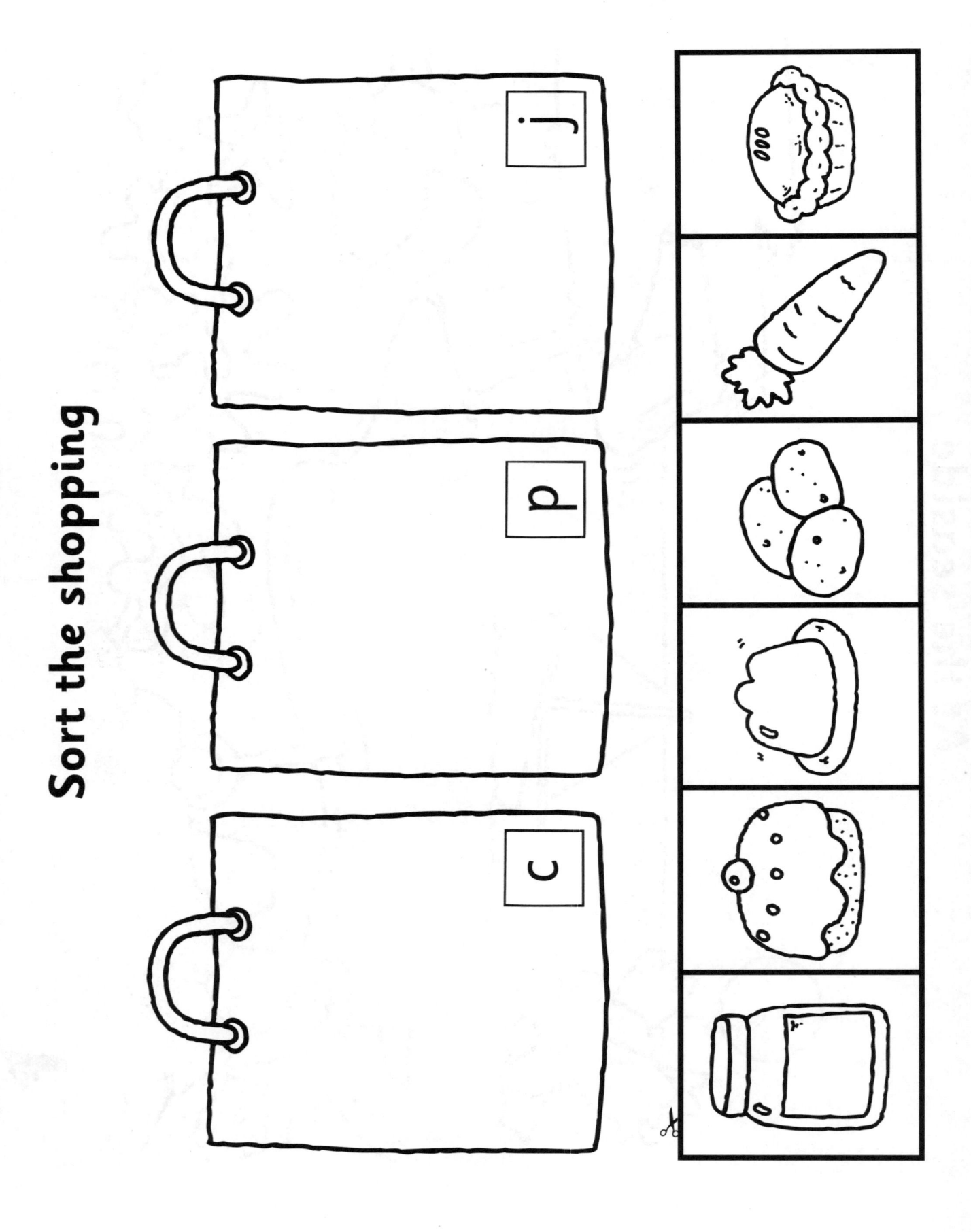

Name

Out and about

Sort the shopping

| j |
| p |
| c |

Communication, Language and Literacy

Name

Out and about

Shopping day

Talk about the picture.

Communication, Language and Literacy

Name _____   **Out and about**

Make a story

Look at the pictures. Talk about what is happening.

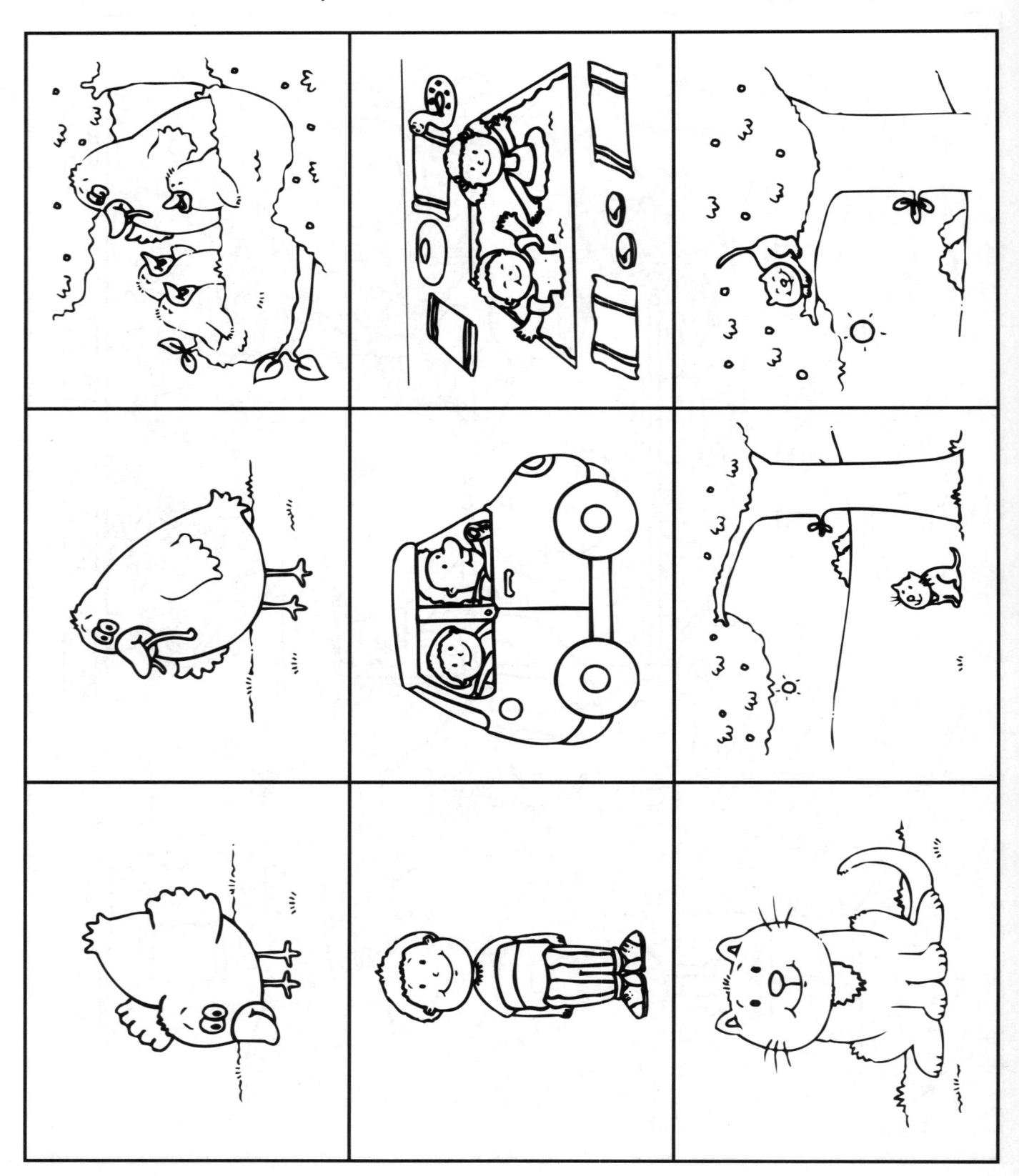

Name

Out and about

A busy park

Look at the picture carefully. Talk about what you can see.

Name   Out and about

Listening lotto

Cover up the sounds when you hear them.

doorbell	traffic
washing	stairs
water	telephone

Name

Out and about

Praying together

What can you see in this picture.
What things do you do with your family?

Name   Out and about

Garages

SpannerGarages Ltd

Name _____

Car _____

Number _____

Work to be done	Cost			

Signed _____

Ministry of Transport Certificate

Car _____

Number _____

Passed/Failed its test _____

Tester's name _____

A sailor went to sea

Use a pencil to follow these waves.

SCHOLASTIC

In this series:

Communication, Language and Literacy
ISBN 0-439-96545-4
ISBN 978-0439-96545-3

Mathematical Development
ISBN 0-439-96546-2
ISBN 978-0439-96546-0

Science – Aspects of Knowledge and Understanding of the World
ISBN 0-439-96547-0
ISBN 978-0439-96547-7

To find out more, call: 0845 603 9091
or visit our website www.scholastic.co.uk